Shooting Through Life

*To Jack Reedy,
With my best wishes and
THANK YOU
for your earlier
encouragement to
guide this book, from the
'Gus'*

Willoughby 'Gus' Gullachsen

12-6-2007.

ISBN 978-09553648 4 6

Published by
Polperro Heritage Press,
Clifton-upon-Teme, Worcestershire WR6 6EN UK
www.polperropress.co.uk

Cover design
Lorentz Gullachsen

Printed by
Orphans Press
Leominster
Herefordshire
United Kingdom

To my friend

EVE

for her help and support in compiling this book

ACKNOWLEDGEMENTS

I would like to thank John Greenwood, Roger Popplestone and Christine Wilkinson for their help and guidance during the course of photographing 189 productions at the old and new Birmingham Repertory theatres.

Thanks are also due to Peter James, Head of Photographs, and Nikki Rathbone of the Shakespeare Studies Department at the Birmingham Central Library, for their kind assistance on many occasions during recent years, and to my friend Jack Reedy whose invaluable help and advice initially gave me the confidence to tackle this enterprise.

I must also mention my appreciation to Nick Hale, Roy Long and Terry Mead for their invaluable support on the many occasions throughout the years when I have carried out assignments for the Central Office of Information, and my gratitude to Malcolm Davies of the Shakespeare Birthplace Trust for his help and advice in recent years.

And last but not least, I must pay tribute to my many friends in the press, broadcasting and television media - some of whom, sadly, are no longer with us - who throughout the years have shown me such warmhearted and generous friendship. It is due to their persuasion and encouragement that I was emboldened to write this book.

CONTENTS

INTRODUCTION

My father was a keen amateur photographer, and as a child I found it fascinating to watch him at work in his darkroom in the cellar of our Edwardian home in Northumberland. He would patiently explain to me the significance of the various liquids which were used for the developing, washing and fixing of negatives.

The years rolled by and soon it was time for me to decide on a career - my thoughts turned to my initial love of photography. I had grown up with photography as a sort of backdrop to my childhood, but until then I had not actually thought of it as a career. Would it be possible, I wondered? Nowadays, of course, it would simply be a matter of applying for a course at a local college or university, but it was a different world in the 1930's. But when an opportunity presented itself in the form of a local commercial photographer looking for someone to train, I convinced him that I was the person he was looking for.

I did not exactly shine in my employer's eyes however, often being clumsy and making silly mistakes. Being a typical teenager, my thoughts were often elsewhere, and after one particularly bad episode, I was dismissed. When my father angrily demanded to know why I had been sacked, my employer replied, "He will never make a photographer!" This was the spur I needed and I became determined to prove him wrong.

Soon I was working for another photographic company, attending the Manchester Technical College in the evenings to acquire more technical knowledge. By February 1939 I was considered competent enough to act as assistant to another photographer at the British Industries Fair. Later, I joined another commercial photographer in the Birmingham area, again in a very junior position, but devoted myself to learning everything possible about my chosen career, and was given every encouragement and plenty of opportunity to develop an all round knowledge of photography, mostly behind the scenes in the processing department, but occasionally even being allowed out on a photographic assignment. I had found my niche.

In the autumn of 1939, war was imminent, and I realized that I would in all probability be called up for war service. Preferring to choose which service I joined, I decided to volunteer rather than wait to be called up, and duly went along to the RAF recruiting office to enlist. At the end of my initial training I attended an interview with a senior officer to decide which sector I should be trained for. I told him I would like to be an RAF photographer. "No, I'm afraid that's not possible," said he, shaking his head. "I'll put you down for an instrument maker." "But sir," I protested, "look at my hands, they are far too large and clumsy for that." "Oh, very well I'll put you down for a photographer," he said impatiently. And so began my RAF career.

Starting in October 1939, a very intensive six months training course followed at the School of RAF Photography in Farnborough, where 1 was given very detailed and thorough training in darkroom work, ground and aerial photography, and cine projection. One whole week was taken to dis-assemble and completely re-assemble a Bell and Howell 16 mm cine projector. Another week to learn the use of a Brownhall mobile photography darkroom. This had 28 stop-cocks, taps and valves; becoming familiar with its use took another full weeks tuition. Practical use in the air with the F24 aerial camera in the nose of an Anson aircraft came at the end of the course after which we were all sent off in different directions. I was posted to Bomber Command, Scampton. On arrival I was informed that I was now ON ACTIVE SERVICE.

A very eventful five years followed, during which I served in South Africa, India and Iraq. After the stimulating, challenging, and often gut-wrenching years of my war service, however, I felt it impossible to face the mundane prospect of starting work again as an employee for a photographic company, so I decided to take a gamble. Using part of my demob money I invested in some darkroom equipment which I installed in the bathroom of my home! My lounge served as a temporary studio. A showcase advertised my work in a nearby shopping centre, and soon requests started to come in for me to photograph weddings, young babies at their parent's homes, etc. and a meagre living began. As time went by, my appointments book was so full, I felt financially secure enough to open a studio.

After a while, the local paper, the West Bromwich *Midland Chronicle* became aware of my work and I was commissioned to take news photographs on their behalf at half a guinea a time. Soon the Birmingham papers began asking for my services and I was flattered when I was asked to work as a local 'stringer' for *Illustrated*, the rival national magazine to *Picture Post*. I had arrived!

I was regularly involved with theatre productions at the Dudley Hippodrome and Birmingham Repertory Theatre and was also frequently asked to do stills photography for ABC TV. In 1966, 'Images of the Sixties', an exhibition of my work, was held in Birmingham. The BBC's Press Officer called in to see it one day, and asked, "Why don't you do work for us?" Thus began my career as a stills photographer.

Looking back over my lifetime working as a photographer, many memories of the people and places I have been lucky enough to have encountered come to mind, from my early portraits of Tembu tribesmen in South Africa while serving with the RAF during the Second World War, through many years of working with famous television personalities in Birmingham, as well as actors and actresses from the many stage and BBC drama productions I worked with over the years. So many, in fact, that the task of selecting just a few for the pages of this book has proved very difficult indeed.

What I have endeavoured to do is choose those images that remind me of some of the many extraordinary events and circumstances I have encountered in the course of my career. Equipped only with my camera, I have been privileged to have worked with people from all walks of life, from members of the Royal family to show business performers at the very beginning of their fame and fortune.

For almost all my work, I have used film but I recently bought a small digital camera and this new technology is wonderful!

NEW STREET STATION

This photograph, taken in 1946, reminds me of a bitterly cold night in the winter of 1940 when I said farewell to my father and settled down in the waiting room at New Street Station, Birmingham to await my early morning train, along with several other servicemen. The waiting room was bleak, with no heating, just an old Victorian fireplace piled high with rubbish. As the night wore on, the cold increased and eventually one of the lads had the bright idea of setting fire to the rubbish in the grate.

We all huddled around the warmth, and soon old newspapers and other material was added until it began to feel quite cosy. However, around 11pm the embers were almost extinguished, and as my train wasn't due until 4.30am the following morning, I decided to go in search of any suitable refuse to keep the fire burning. The air raid siren went off during my search, but this was more or less routine at that time, and I didn't pay much attention. Soon I had gathered a few old cardboard packing cases and newspapers and returning triumphant to the waiting room, pushed aside the wartime blackout curtain to be met by a cloud of smoke and steam.

Through the murk I saw one or two firemen and, horror of horrors, a red cap military policeman. "And what are you going to do with that rubbish?" he barked.

"Er, well I was going to re-kindle the fire to warm up the room," I stammered.

"Do you realize what you have done?"

"No," I replied.

"Well come with me and I'll show you." I followed obediently, and walking to the end of the platform he pointed to the chimney which was blazing away like a firework display. And this in the middle of an air raid warning!

"You are on a charge. What is you number, rank and name? You will be hearing more about this."

My case awaits!

TRANSKEI

During the Second World War I spent two years on RAF service as a photographer in South Africa based at Queenstown. When off duty, I would occasionally take my camera with me to photograph the people of the Transkei territory in the Eastern Cape.

It was on one such trip in 1941 that I was able to capture this portrait of a magnificent Tembu witch doctor. I considered it one of my best shots of that period and it subsequently won first prize in a local Queenstown photographic competition.

Red filter 5x 1/50 F8 Panatonic X

THE GULF OF OMAN

I served in the RAF during the Second World War and was stationed at Shar-jah in Trucial Oman in 1942, when I was startled one day to hear a loud explosion on the far side of the airfield in the vicinity of the aviation fuel depot. Seconds later, it was a horrifying sight as dense, black smoke clouds engulfed the area.

Grabbing a nearby F24 aerial camera, I raced to the scene and recorded the incident. An ambulance can be seen in the foreground en route to the fire, but sadly nothing could be done for the four Arab Levies who were guarding the storage depot which contained 28,000 gallons of high octane fuel. The fire blazed for some 24 hours before it was brought under control.

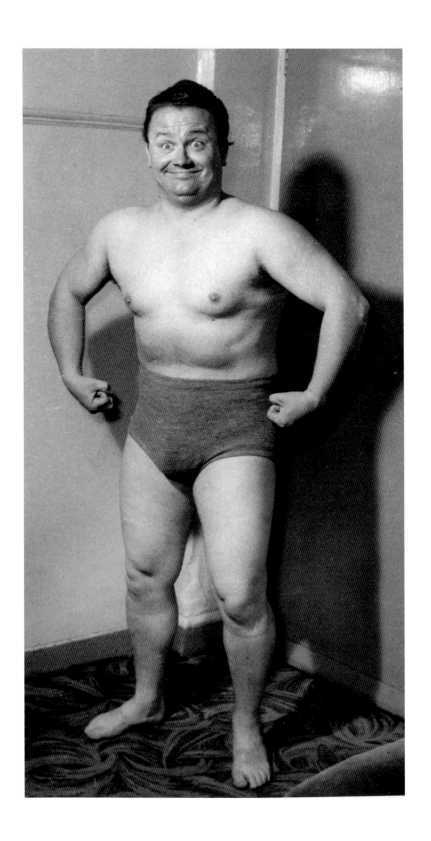

HARRY SECOMBE

Harry Secombe was appearing at the Dudley Hippodrome in the 1950s when he was asked if he would perform the opening of a new discotheque in a cellar in New Street, Birmingham, and sign his latest HMV record release *Heart of a Clown*.

On the morning arranged, his new Austin Atlantic pulled up nearby, but little advance publicity had resulted in a very poor attendance. I bought a record myself, which Sir Harry kindly autographed for me.

The manager and his assistant were present, and after the manager had discreetly rewarded Harry for his appearance, he turned to the chauffeur: "Do pick a record," and pointed to several displayed on the walls nearby.

"I would like that one," he quickly replied, pointing to a recording of Gustaf Holst's *Planets Suite*. The chauffeur accepted the record and slipped quietly away unrecognised. Nothing more to relate, except that the chauffeur's name was Peter Sellars!

SPIKE MILLIGAN

While I was photographing Harry Secombe for publicity purposes at the Dudley Hippodrome in the 1950s, his old friend Spike Milligan called in to visit him. Though I had no particular reason at that time to photograph this eccentric character, his natural wit and humour were so compelling, the words just flowing out with such speed, I felt that perhaps a quick shot of him would be interesting. I instinctively reacted when I saw his wacky look in my direction.

I'm glad to have recorded this unique character. A comic genius, his like is rarely seen.

THE BEATLES

In the early 1960s, before they became internationally famous, the 'Fab Four' were invited to appear on *Thank Your Lucky Stars* at the Alpha Television Studios in Birmingham, and on the day they were due to perform I was on duty as the stills photographer.

They had appeared at the studios some weeks previously and word had obviously got round among the local teenagers that they were back. The streets near the studios were crowded with fans - there were literally hundreds of young girls. I had to park my car some distance away and use a rugby scrum strategy to make my way to the stage door. One young lady resented my approach and used her stiletto heel on my foot to register her disapproval. Undeterred, I limped painfully on my way to the stage door entrance.

Later on that afternoon, as I was about to take the stills photographs of the *Thank Your Lucky Stars* production, Paul McCartney asked me what I was doing (the days of the paparazzi had not yet arrived). I explained that I was there to take publicity photos for the production and within the next few days the company would notify the media, which would result in greater public awareness. He seemed satisfied to learn that any photos published would help the group's career.

PETULA CLARKE

This very popular singer had agreed to appear as a guest star on ABC TV's *Thank Your Lucky Stars* while on a visit to the U.K. from her home in France.

However, by the time of the rehearsal Petula was in an advanced stage of pregnancy. This presented something of a dilemma - in the 1960s attitudes were not as liberal as they are today, and it would have been considered not quite decorous for ladies to perform in public in 'a certain condition'.

The director came up with the idea of photographing her sitting behind the wheel of an open-top sports car, thus focusing all the attention on her face. This worked very well, as by the clever use of a moving backdrop of scenery, she appeared to be driving the car along a country road although it was actually stationary in the studio.

I think the resulting photo captures the vivacity and charm of this very talented singer.

J. B. PRIESTLEY

My first encounter with J. B. Priestley was many years ago when I had a call from Peter Green who had become the Editor of *TV World*. "Meet me at J. B. Priestley's near Stratford upon Avon." As Peter interviewed the famous author and World War II radio personality, I listened to their conversation from a respectful distance of some ten feet away.

I knew that Peter would greatly appreciate a picture of the two of them as they talked in the garden of Kissing Tree Cottage. I clicked the shutter, whereupon Priestley, who was smoking his briar pipe, hearing the sound, turned and gave a severe and withering look straight at the offensive camera lens. Fortunately I had wound on and was ready for this supreme and definitive moment.

Many years later a call from Anglia TV requested my presence at the home of the great man. At 3pm precisely the front door was opened by Mrs Priestley who led myself and the film crew down a long corridor to the library at the end of their sumptuous home. Soon the lighting technicians got to work assembling their equipment. After a few minutes J. B. Priestley himself appeared. He was, of course, much older and after some difficulty settled himself into a tall upright leather upholstered chair. My moment to cover this well lit occasion had arrived and I took colour transparencies, and black and white material which was later surrendered to Anglia TV.

The interview began. "Tell me, Mr Priestley, you knew Max Miller. What was he like?" After a puff on his pipe, he replied: "Well, he was suggestive". After this brief rehearsal the director/interviewer checked the team – 'camera running, sound running – action!'

The previous question regarding Max Miller was repeated and the reply came quickly. "He was suggestive." Having muttered these few words, the interview was expected to continue but the great author leant forward and looked at the carpet. Half a minute went by, but the expected revelations about Max Miller, though eagerly anticipated, were not forthcoming.

Another few seconds went by, whilst the anxious crew looked at each other. The TV camera was still running, the frustrated director looked concerned – the top of Priestley's head was, alas, unmoving After two or three minutes more of inactivity we all understood that sadly, old age had caught up with the subject of our attention. The director called out "That's it – it's a wrap!"

LULU

In the early 1960s I was commissioned by ABC TV to photograph the production of *Thank Your Lucky Stars* which was recorded on Sunday for transmission the following Saturday evening.

One Sunday morning I arrived to cover the dress rehearsal as usual and some way through the rehearsals a young lady arrived rather late, and with no time to change into her stage costume. She was calm and composed and appeared to be not in the least unnerved by the situation and went straight into her performance. The minute this Scots lass began to sing, I was struck by the power of her voice and I noticed that several of the studio crew were taken aback and temporarily stopped work to enjoy listening, and were fascinated as she swayed her hips to the rhythm of the music. It was an electrifying performance, particularly from one so young. I believe she was 16 years old at the time. The tune was of course *Shout* which became a great hit, and she was soon on her way to the top.

It was a moment to capture, and of course I had my camera at hand.

ADAM FAITH

One day, whilst working on the Sunday afternoon recordings of the ABC television series *Thank Your Lucky Stars* I was intrigued to see an original set that displayed several prominent individual images of Adam Faith. I photographed this just for the record, not really believing that there would be any PR use for it.

Some six months later Adam Faith returned to the studio and stood in front of this large black and white print blow-up of the earlier photograph. I took the opportunity of photographing this unusual shot, a reproduction of which I later used in my 'In Focus' middle page spread which appeared monthly in the sadly now defunct *Birmingham Sketch*.

ARNOLD WESKER

Chips With Everything, one of Arnold Wesker's most successful plays, was showing at the Birmingham Repertory Theatre, and hearing that the gifted playwright was to visit the theatre I phoned the press officer, Chris Wilkinson, to see if I could arrange a visit. She was most helpful, and arranged a lunchtime photo session for me.

On meeting the playwright, I assured him that there would be an opportunity for him to approve my pictures and that I would destroy any which he did not want published. During the session, as a change from an ordinary portrait, I decided to fit a multiple prism on the lens of my Nikon, and he was delighted with the resulting picture.

SHIRLEY BASSEY

My first photographs of Shirley Bassey were taken as she was leaving a Birmingham hospital one Sunday morning. At that time she was relatively unknown, and so far as I was concerned it was just a routine photograph assignment. Little did I realize then that with her talent and personality she would go on to captivate audiences for decades. We met again when she appeared with conductor/composer Geoff Love on the late night show *After Hours*, and it was obvious then that she had a brilliant career ahead of her.

Many singers presented themselves very casually for dress rehearsal before the final take, but she always appeared smartly dressed and fully made up, as for the final take, which made my work much easier.

Much later on, when she was appearing in the BBC's *Pebble Mill at One* lunchtime programme, I again needed to photograph her, and waited quietly in the wings to photograph her with Alan Titchmarsh, the presenter.

The programme ended, and as I walked across the studio floor the studio lights went out. A new lighting director, unaware of my need for lighting, had gone to lunch. I approached Alan and Shirley and explained what had happened.

"I'm afraid I will have to use flash."

Shirley looked me in the eye: "OK – I love flashers," she said with a smile.

MICHAEL BENTINE

I was working in London in my capacity as an ACCT stills photographer in the 1960s when I first met Michael Bentine. We established a rapport almost immediately when we discovered we had each served in the RAF during the war.

Michael was enjoying great success appearing in that famous radio comedy series *The Goon Show*, with Peter Sellars, Harry Secombe, and Spike Milligan.

We met again some time later when I was the stills photographer on the Saturday evening ABC TV show *After Hours*, in which Michael was appearing, and our friendship developed still further when we found that we had a mutual interest in art.

The television company suggested that Michael and I should stage a joint exhibition, showing my photos and Michael's sketches of the *After Hours* cast. This we agreed to do - we had a great time putting the show together and it proved to be a huge success.

One day Michael asked if I would do some studio publicity photos for him, and it was whilst we were working on these that Michael mentioned that his son was interested in photography and asked if it would be possible for me to take him on as an apprentice. Regretfully, I had to refuse as I was planning to offer the opportunity to my own son when the time was right.

Sadly, Michael's son was killed some years later in a tragic air crash. He and a friend had chartered a plane to watch the *Daily Express* Off-Shore Motor Boat Race, and the plane did not return. It was not until three months later that the wreckage was found in a forest. Michael was later instrumental in pioneering the action by the Civil Aviation Authority in instructing that in future no aircraft were allowed to take off without disclosing their destination.

Nikon 105 mm F.8 1/250th Nikon

CHRIS TARRANT

Chris Tarrant and I had agreed to have lunch at Valentino's (a restaurant famed for its delicious steaks) in Harborne, Birmingham, to discuss my photographic involvement in forthcoming productions of his popular Saturday programme *Tiswas*.

We were joined by the show's writer and director and details of highlights in various forthcoming scenes were gone into, involving celebrities who were to be surprised with some unexpected events during the live Saturday production ahead. Foreknowledge of these often explosive moments was invaluable since they enabled me to be in a safe place on the studio floor at the right time.

After an excellent meal, accompanied by wine, during which I had drunk large quantities of iced water, it was time for us to return to the ATV studios in Bridge Street. But first I had to answer an urgent call of nature, so made my way to the gents cloakroom. Alas, the only loo was occupied. Chris reminded me that they had to leave as soon as possible; we had lingered too long over our meal, and the writer and director were becoming anxious. "We have to return now," said Chris sharply. As I was driving them, I had no choice but to leave immediately.

As we headed for the studios I was getting more and more uncomfortable, and looked desperately from side to side for somewhere, perhaps even a secluded garden hedge, to answer the call of nature. It was during this left, right search that I unfortunately failed to observe a red traffic light at a crossroads! There was a collision with a car crossing the junction from the other direction — fortunately no-one was injured, although we were all considerably shaken.

A taxi took Chris and his team back to the studios, whilst I dashed into the nearby Chamber of Commerce where at last I found a place for relief. Later, sitting in a police car, I had to recount in detail the moments leading to the collision. I duly admitted the offence, pleading extenuating circumstances! I was subsequently fined and my driving licence endorsed.

A harsh lesson but a right one. There could well have been no *Who Wants To Be A Millionaire*.

TED MOULT

In addition to being a working farmer, Ted Moult excelled himself in his performances on the popular BBC *Brains Trust* programme, and was already a well known personality by the time I first met him. Not only was he extremely knowledgeable, but his wit and dry sense of humour, together with his genial smile, had endeared him to thousands.

I had been asked to take some stills photographs for the media prior to his appearance on ITV, and on arriving at his farm near Ashbourne in Derbyshire, I enquired of his whereabouts. His wife pointed out a figure in a distant field. I made my way over the fields to where he was working and introduced myself. "I'm too busy now for photographs," he growled dismissively. Not to be put off by this unexpected outburst, I placed my camera case on the ground, took off my coat and began helping him to move the heavy bags of potatoes he was loading onto a truck. A short time later, with the job finished, his true nature re-asserted itself when he invited me back to the farmhouse for a cuppa. I was introduced to his wife and children and soon we were all chatting away lightheartedly. I took a family group photograph before doing the official photograph of this charming and brainy character, and said my farewells.

I did not realize then that I was to see him often when he appeared several times on the *Tiswas* programme, and I photographed him frequently for ATV's publicity purposes.

Time went by, and one day as I was driving back to my Birmingham studio, I was stunned to hear the radio announcement of his suicide. I must admit I rarely shed a tear, but as I listened to that radio bulletin I was considerably choked. He was a man's man, a very generous and thoughtful personality, and all who knew him were deeply saddened by his inexplicable end.

SUE NICHOLLS

On a visit to the Houses of Parliament to photograph Midlands MPs, I unexpectedly met Lord Harmer Nicholls who had called into the House of Commons for lunch.

On being introduced, I asked him if his daughter was Sue Nicholls, the actress, at that time appearing in the ATV soap *Crossroads* and whose publicity photograph I had taken. He replied that indeed she was, and confirmed his pride in his daughter's success in the popular television series.

Shortly afterwards, the talented actress moved to Granada's *Coronation Street*, where for many years she has delighted audiences with her performance as one of the leading characters in this evergreen soap.

BARRY FOSTER

In the late 1970s I was asked if I was available to go and work as the stills photographer on a Children's Film Foundation movie, *Danger on Dartmoor*.

The invitation came at a very opportune moment as there was an industrial dispute at ATV in Birmingham at the time, which meant I had plenty of time on my hands. I needed no further bidding and packed my gear and, most importantly in view of the location, a well-used Barbour raincoat and a pair of wellies. Little did I realise how important these boots were going to be.

Arriving at my hotel in Chagford in the early evening, I was introduced to the crew who were settled in a quiet, dimly lit corner of the bar. I noticed that each and every one of them was holding a small glass containing a creamy brownish liquid.

"What on earth is that?" I enquired. "Why, it's Baileys. Try one." Over the following days I was suitably fortified with this newly discovered and tasty liqueur.

The raw, damp cold on Dartmoor has to be experienced to be believed, and during the next few days I certainly needed my Barbour. To my relief I found that an old and long-disused cottage was to be the main interior location. My relief was short-lived however. Over the years hundreds of sheep had found shelter in this old building, and had left behind several inches of their droppings… I was very glad I had brought my wellies along!

Barry Foster was more than convincing in his role as an escaped convict, shivering for real as he hid behind a large rock while sheltering from the rain - and he certainly needed fortification in the bar that evening along with myself and the rest of the crew.

YSANNE CHURCHMAN

For many years Ysanne Churchman played the part of Grace Archer in the popular BBC radio programme *The Archers*, devised by Godfrey Baseley. Many thousands tuned in each evening to hear the latest developments in this popular family saga. *The Archers* is now the longest running radio programme in the world.

However, in 1955 the start of commercial television was seen as a possible threat to the listening figures. Drastic action had to be taken to keep the listeners glued to their radios, and what could be more compelling than a fire at Brookfields Farm. The listeners were riveted to their sets as the drama unfolded, and it became obvious that Grace's life was in danger. Sadly, the character was killed in the fire, to the great distress of many listeners, with whom Grace was a much-loved character. But the story line had the desired effect, resulting in wide media coverage and taking some of the limelight away from the launch of ITV.

HUGH CARLTON GREENE

It was a momentous occasion when in 1970 the then Director-General of the BBC, Sir Hugh Carlton Greene cut the first sod prior to building commencing on BBC Pebble Mill.

An audience of BBC executives watched as his spade cut through the turf with effortless ease. I learned later that the BBC gardener had loosened the hard soil in advance - wise advance planning.

Sad to reflect that some 30 years later the building was considered outmoded and has since been demolished.

GERALD NABARRO

I had several different studios during the course of my career, but undoubtedly my favourite was located on Hagley Road in a row of the only existing Regency houses in Birmingham. The two ground floor rooms made an excellent studio and office, while the basement provided a very useful workroom with separate darkroom.

Over the years, many of the Midlands most beautiful girls were sent from the Olive Carpenter Model Agency to be photographed by me. The resulting prints portrayed the model in four different poses, wearing different outfits, and illustrated the girls' ability to display the clothes to the best advantage.

In addition, a great many young actors and actresses from the Birmingham Repertory Theatre, the BBC and ABC studios came along to be photographed.

One morning, there was a very loud rat-a-tat on the front door knocker which demanded immediate attention. On answering it, I was confronted by the tall and flamboyant figure of the Midlands MP Sir Gerald Nabarro who informed me in a booming voice that he required to be photographed. Well known for his eccentric tendencies and ostentatious lifestyle, he was quite a change from my usual clients.

MORECAMBE & WISE

I met Eric Morecambe for the first time when the pair were playing nightly to packed houses at the Dudley Hippodrome in the 1960s; I was there to record Eric's visit to an opticians in Cradley Heath where he was presented with a pair of spectacles. I later met Ernie Wise when he was my guest for lunch during a promotion of my 'Biz and Showbiz' exhibition in Birmingham in the 1970s.

We met again when they were performing in the opening show of the newly built Princess Theatre in Torquay, and I had the task - when I could manage to stop myself from shaking with laughter - of taking several publicity photographs of these memorable comedians.

Many encounters were to follow over the years, and they never failed to amuse with their natural wit. Both on stage and off, they were so much in tune with each other. This unforgettable duo have left a big gap in British comedy entertainment - they are sadly missed.

DEREK JACOBI

Derek Jacobi came to my Birmingham studio in the early 1970s to be photographed while he was playing the lead in *Oedopus Rex* at the Birmingham Repertory Theatre. I had been enthralled by his performance when I covered the dress rehearsal earlier and Midlands audiences had certainly shown their approval of this production of the Greek tragedy, which is believed to be the world's oldest play.

Glancing outside, I saw that the weather was bright after an earlier shower of rain, so rather than use the traditional studio lighting, I decided a more original background could be found in the garden of my studio. Using a long lens to throw the background out of focus, I used a nearby tree as a prop, and Mother Nature provided a suitable frontal lighting with bright afternoon sunlight.

As time went by, Derek's career blossomed, and he was awarded a knighthood for his talented performances in the theatre.

FRANCES PITT

"Who was the most interesting person you have ever photographed?" the BBC Midlands radio presenter Ed Doolan asked me when he interviewed me on air in the 1970s. I had no hesitation in replying, "Frances Pitt".

A highly respected naturalist, writer and photographer, she was a pioneer of wildlife photography. Many of her nature photographs were published many years before I was born in 1921, and I was pleased to have the opportunity of photographing her at her home near Much Wenlock when I was looking for a good subject for my In Focus column in the *Birmingham Sketch* in the early 60s.

We both shared a love of nature and photography, but she had worked in a different era to myself. Her photographs were taken using an old bellows camera and she needed extreme patience to obtain the wonderful photographs she produced. Patience is all important when photographing wildlife; I doubt whether I would have had the forbearance and tenacity to achieve such results. She could have taught me a great deal.

Whilst chatting I discovered that she was a lady of very varied interests. I was surprised to learn that she had once been the Master of the Shrewsbury Hunt. On display in the sitting room was a pair of fighting cocks' spurs, often used in days gone by in secretive meetings, as cock fighting was banned. I commented that they were an unexpected thing to find in a nature lover's home. With a smile she told me that they were a gift from her friend Phil Drabble, the presenter of the BBC television series *One Man and His Dog*.

But the thing I found most intriguing was the pair of Albino squirrels that she kept as pets in her home. They were completely tame, and lived indoors in pretty much the same manner as a pet cat would. The photograph shows her giving 'Mr Nuts' a favourite treat - he really was as white as the driven snow, a most amazing sight.

ALEC ISSIGONIS

Arriving for my appointment to photograph Sir Alec Issigonis, I was driving, rather appropriately I thought, a Morris Minor shooting brake of which I had recently become the proud owner. Appropriate, because, although he was best known as the designer of the Mini, he also designed the Morris Minor and the Austin 1100.

Feeling somewhat in awe of the great engineer and designer, I was shown into his office but was soon put at ease. He was a charming man, and one of the easiest subjects I have ever encountered - a pleasure to photograph. His modesty was apparent when I referred to his brainchild the Mini, and it was at this point that my shutter clicked.

When asked to take a portrait, one of the things I like to do is capture the essential nature of the subject, and I feel that in this photo of Sir Alec I have achieved that.

DONALD WOLFIT

It was with some trepidation that I approached Sir Donald Wolfit when he appeared on an ABC TV production, due to his reputation as one of the great actor/managers of the theatre whose stage career began in 1920. During the Second World War his company presented over 100 lunchtime performances to war-torn Britain.

Immediately after taking this photograph I retreated quickly from the set, lest I be subjected to one of his sudden and unexpected rebukes for which he was famous

JEAN ANDERSON

Jean Anderson was one of the leading character actresses of her generation. She was extremely talented and versatile, appearing in a wide variety of roles on stage, screen and television.

I best remember her for her role as the matriarchal grandmother who stirred the family into action in *The Brothers*, the hugely successful TV drama recorded at BBC Pebble Mill in the 1970s. Her acting expertise livened up each episode. During tea breaks I was privileged to meet this lady who was rarely out of work since leaving RADA.

Many years passed until we met again on a BBC drama production location near Stafford. With the passing years her warm personality had not changed, and it was a pleasure to photograph her again. She continued acting right up until a few months before her death at the grand old age of 93 in 2001.

She was loved and respected by all who knew her.

MIKE YARWOOD

Mike Yarwood was a superb impressionist who was able to mimic many well-known personalities of the day. I went backstage when he was appearing at the Coventry Hippodrome, and persuaded him to be photographed between performances. I wanted to capture him in the character of the people he was then impersonating, and I like to think that I succeeded. I managed to take quite a few shots before he had to go back on stage. A very talented man.

KEN DODD

I was first introduced to Ken Dodd by his publicist George Bartram at Aston Villa football club over 50 years ago.

Since that initial introduction I have had the pleasure of photographing Ken on numerous occasions, and we have come to know each other quite well over the years.

In the 1970s I was staging a photography exhibition in Birmingham – 'Biz and Showbiz' – in which a photograph of Ken was featured, and as Ken was appearing at the Coventry Hippodrome at the time, he very kindly agreed to come along to see the exhibition. He had a very busy schedule, so we arranged that I would pick him up at the Leofric Hotel where he was staying and drive him to the exhibition. At the appointed time I arrived at the hotel, but there was no sign of Ken. When he eventually arrived, I had to push my Austin A40 to its limits, but we did manage to get to Birmingham in time for our lunch appointment.

Ken has enthralled thousands of people throughout the years with his quixotic and effervescent brand of humour. There are few comedians who have captured the public affection over such a long period of time. But not only is he a great comedian, he is also very versatile, as he demonstrated when he appeared in Kenneth Branagh's screen version of *Hamlet*. He also played the part of Malvolio in Shakespeare's *Twelfth Night* at the Liverpool Playhouse some time ago. Quite recently he gave a talk at the Royal Shakespeare Theatre in Stratford when he discussed the meaning of humour. Shakespeare could, I am sure, have woven his character into one of his plays!

Some time later, when he was appearing on stage at the Alexandra Theatre in Birmingham, I met him in his dressing room and asked him if he would come to a Birmingham Press Club lunch during his stay.

"Of course, what's in it for me?"

We settled on twelve bottles of wine!

1/125 flash on camera fill in F.8 1/125 Fuji colour

JUDI DENCH

It was the day of Shakespeare's Birthday Celebrations, and I was strolling along enjoying the April sunshine. On this occasion I decided to join the Annual Birthday Parade later just before Hall's Croft, as an old leg injury was causing me some discomfort. As I approached Hall's Croft (where Shakespeare's daughter Susanna had lived with her husband Dr John Hall) a voice called out "Hello Gus". It was Ann Kenyon, the Chief Guide at Hall's Croft.

I turned round to acknowledge her and to my surprise, seated just a few feet away were two very well known actors watching the parade go by. My camera was ready and, quickly looking through the zoom lens, I recorded Dame Judi Dench and her husband Michael Williams. They were totally unaware of this, being engrossed in watching the parade go by. Some years earlier, when working as a stills photographer for ATV, I was lucky enough to cover a recording of *Comedy of Errors* in which Michael and Dame Judi were memorable.

When this candid camera shot was developed I felt that it had perfectly captured their personalities, and put it into my collection for possible future use. Sadly, some time later we were to hear of Michael's premature death. In due course I received a phone call from *Shakespeare at the Centre* magazine consultant Jack Reedy, requesting a close-up of Michael for use on the front cover of the magazine, in which they paid a tribute to this very talented actor.

LARRY GRAYSON

For more than 30 years Larry, who was brought up in Nuneaton, toured the clubs and music halls, mostly in the North and Midlands, doing his drag act. By the time I met him in the 1970s he was a top star, having got his 'break' when he appeared on ATV's *Saturday Variety Show*. He went on to be voted *TV Times* Funniest Man of the Year, and later topped the bill at the London Palladium.

He was especially popular with viewing audiences in the Midlands, and his catchphrase 'shut that door' was on everybody's lips. Included in his act were stories full of innuendo about the antics of a group of imaginary characters, Everard, Slack Alice, Apricot Lil and Co. had his audiences convulsed with laughter.

I was contacted one day by Larry's manager, Paul Vaughan, who asked me to take a colour photograph of Larry to illustrate the cover of his new book, based on the imaginary exploits of his television characters in World War Two. Suitable garments were required to portray Larry as an air raid warden – I managed to acquire a traditional tin hat, whilst Paul provided the duffle coat and gas mask.

As an ex-BBC employee Paul knew of a suitable location at the rear of the redundant BBC premises in Broad Street, Birmingham, a site now occupied by the towering Hyatt Hotel building.

Much later, when the book was published, I acquired a copy, and having lived through the 1939-45 conflict I was doubled up with laughter at the antics of Slack Alice and her associates.

SIMON KIRBY

I am a member of the Stratford Society, a group formed to ensure the preservation and enhancement of all that is good in the town. Some years ago, I was asked if I would like to take Simon Kirby's place in a group of members who were engaged in photographing all of the main streets of this ancient town, as he had recently acquired the business of Thomas Crapper Ltd, a firm famous for its decorated lavatory pedestals since Victorian times, and could no longer spare the time for the photography.

Sometime later I had reason to visit him at his business premises in the grounds of nearby Alscot House, the home of the Weston family. His offices were crammed full of what must be a unique collection of early lavatory pedestals, in which setting I had planned to photograph Simon.

While chatting about these antique pedestals he mentioned that he was also interested in penny farthing bicycles and it transpired that he actually owned one which he had learned to ride. Of course I could not resist this opportunity for an unusual photo for my forthcoming exhibition.

It took quite some time to achieve, as the right weather conditions for the shot had to coincide with Simon being free from business commitments on the day, but eventually we succeeded, and the resulting photograph was ultimately used to publicise my 2005 exhibition 'Around Stratford Town'.

THE QUEEN MOTHER

For some time I had been keen to show that many people continue to lead a very busy and fulfilling life long after the age of retirement.

To this end, in 1998, after discussions with Peter James, Head of Photographs at Birmingham Central Library, it was agreed that I should produce 50 photographs of people aged 65 years young who had defied the passage of time and, instead of recognising their age by putting their feet up and relaxing, had continued to live life to the full. I was fortunate in receiving financial support from both the BBC and ATV, Saga, Fuji Films and others in order to stage the exhibition *Senior Citizens* in 2000.

Near the completion of this work, I realized that there was one very special elderly person who should be included. The 98th birthday of the Queen Mother was imminent! I wrote to the Clarence House Press Office to ask if they could confirm that her regular appearance outside Clarence House was a possibility, and received a reply that the Royal appearance was indeed possible but not definite.

On arrival outside Clarence House, I joined the throng of news reporters and photographers outside the gates and prepared for a long wait. At 9.00am the tall gates opened slightly and I and other approved photographers were directed to go behind a barrier placed opposite the main entrance where we stayed tightly crammed for the next two hours.

Some colleagues had brought aluminium ladders and used them to hopefully gain an unobstructed view of the wonderful lady who appeared smiling at exactly 11am to the tumultuous cheering of well-wishers. A long procession of children then appeared to present her with bouquets and wish her well. Every child's tribute was received with a charming smile and handed to a palace attendant. My shutter clicked continuously, hoping for that special moment.

300mm Nikkor on Nikon T8 1/20 F11 Fuji colour

PERCY THROWER

Many thousands of viewers tune in each week to watch the popular gardening programmes on offer, such as *Gardeners' World* and *The Flying Gardener*, but in the days of black and white television, Percy Thrower was unchallenged in his unique gardening slot on BBC television. The programme was produced by Barry Edgar, who was also the producer of the popular television show *Come Dancing*, for which he was awarded the prestigious Carl Allen award.

My first encounter with Percy was at his garden in Shrewsbury, which was the location for the programmes. I arrived, unpacked my cameras and waited for the rehearsal to begin. Producer Barry Edgar was nearby when Percy was given the cue to start. I was impressed when he immediately started talking confidently about the vegetable produce in front of him. He continued discussing the produce for a good few minutes, never wavering or pausing throughout the entire rehearsal. Here indeed, was a true professional; he really knew his subject. It is little wonder that for many years the viewing figures were so impressive.

In the years that followed, many viewers learned how to care for their gardens through watching Percy's 'down-to-earth' demonstrations on how to dig, plant, prune and generally care for their plots.

From Kodachrome 1/66 F 6.3

VENICE

In 1970 I was one of a group of people visiting Venice for a few days at the invitation of the Italian tourist authorities in order to promote tourism in the area. Venice is a photographers paradise - so many wonderful sights, it is little wonder that camera toting tourists flock there from all over the world.

Having a few moments to myself one day I was looking around for a subject which was perhaps a little different from the obvious, when my eye was attracted to the four bronze horses positioned high up on St. Mark's Basilica. Making my way to a suitable vantage point, I was about to take the shot when suddenly a man's head appeared in view which served to give proportion to these bronze horse replicas which were brought to Venice in the year 1204.

The final day of our visit had been hot and humid, and it was with some relief that we made our way back to the hotel where a special meal was being prepared for us as we were leaving the following morning. Just as we were about to start eating the lights went out, but waiters quickly appeared carrying lighted candles which they placed on the table. Just as they did so the lights came on again, much to everyone's amusement. The atmosphere was happy and relaxed but it soon became obvious that a pretty bad storm was brewing. High winds had sprung up, rattling the windows like castanets, and within minutes the storm was raging overhead. As we continued with our meal, we heard police sirens and the sound of ambulances going by and assumed that they were answering emergency calls due to the storm. We were totally unaware of the tragedy that was unfolding in the vicinity.

It was not until we arrived back in England that I heard the tragic news that 70 people had been drowned in the lagoon when a ferry had been overturned during the storm by a tornado.

My wife Doris was considerably relieved when I arrived home safely as she had read reports of the disaster in the *Birmingham Evening Mail*.

CECILY BERRY

Cecily Berry has been Voice Director of the Royal Shakespeare Company in Stratford upon Avon since joining the company in 1969, and her work involves voice training both in Stratford and London, together with work with various touring companies and tuition in schools, working with both teachers and students.

A modest lady, always keeping a low profile, she is a highly respected and valued member of the company, and her ability to 'speak the spoken word' has taken her around the world, working with theatre companies abroad, including the United States, India, Australia and many European countries. She was one of the guest speakers at the annual Shakespeare Birthday lunch a few years ago, and her clear and melodious voice was a delight to listen to.

When I was commissioned by the Birmingham Library to do an exhibition entitled *Senior Citizens*, featuring characters who were 65 years 'young' and continuing to put something extra into their lives after the usual retirement age, I felt that Cecily Berry would be an ideal candidate for the exhibition. When I contacted her she very kindly agreed to pose for this photograph outside 'The Other Place' in Stratford on her way to work.

GODFREY BASELEY

Although Godfrey Baseley was a BBC Midlands Producer for many years he is best known for his brainchild, BBC radios's *The Archers*, the most popular and longest running radio serial, broadcast nationally from 1951.

I had worked with him on several occasions in earlier years, but in the early 1970s we worked together more closely when the BBC commissioned me to take photographs for what was to be the *Borchester Echo*, a newspaper depicting the lives of the people of Ambridge, and also stories of the actors who played them.

Godfrey was responsible for the compilation of the programme, and a list of instructions duly arrived from him. It was a revelation to me during the weeks that followed when he educated me in various farming matters. Each Monday morning throughout that summer I drove to his home in Tewkesbury where he would be waiting to drive me in his Rover 90 to different venues around the Midlands.

A trip to the Royal Agricultural show at Stoneleigh was followed by visits to numerous farms in the West Midlands which involved me in photographing mother pigs and their litters, apple orchards, chicken farms, hunting hounds and horses, sheep and cows. A variety of farming methods were also included on the list of photographs required.

It was a delight to collaborate with Godfrey on this project, and I learnt an enormous amount about country life from him. Everything had to be right; he was precise and professional, an excellent producer, but also a countryman at heart - he obviously loved the programme and all that it stood for.

HUGH GRIFFITH

The British actor Hugh Griffith won an Oscar for his performance as the slave master in the 1959 award winning film *Ben Hur*, and as a result he was invited to appear on the ATV television programme *Midland Profile*. I accompanied the programmes researcher George Bartram on a visit to his home in the Cotswolds, in order to make the necessary arrangements.

As it was a lovely summer's day he invited us out into his beautiful garden where a table was laid for afternoon tea. He was a very charming and relaxed host as he kindly poured each of us a refreshing cup of tea.

As we chatted, he asked what the fee would be for his appearance on the programme, and when told the princely sum of £25 was the usual fee there was a deathly silence for a moment or two. I imagine this was in stark contrast to the fee he had earned for his performance in *Ben Hur*! However, he agreed to appear but felt it was too risky to park his new Daimler in the city centre, so it was arranged that he would leave it on the outskirts of town and the studio would arrange for him to be collected from there and conveyed to the studio.

HONOR BLACKMAN

By the time Independent Television began I had acquired a union card which stated that I was a stills photographer and member of the Association of Cinema and Television Technicians.

One of the regular requirements in my work was to record television sets, prints of which were supplied as a future guide to the various crews in order for them to light, assemble and accurately place properties, bookshelves, ornaments, pictures etc. so that correct continuity could be observed, sometimes weeks later.

On one occasion, after completing a record of a set I called into the Green Room, which in the early sixties also served as a make-up room. To my surprise, there was Honor Blackman in the process of being made-up prior to a television appearance. I told her about my work and asked her permission to take a still photograph whilst she was being made up. I also took a separate portrait of her, once her make-up was complete.

Later this lovely lady was to be internationally recognized as Pussy Galore in the James Bond film *Goldfinger*.

BEN TRAVERS

Shortly before the curtain was raised at the Birmingham Repertory Theatre on the first night of the Ben Travers comedy, *After You With the Milk*, I was tipped off by the theatre administrator, John Greenwood, that the famous playwright was in the front of house bar. It would be a catch if I could seize the opportunity to take this 90-year-old gentleman, who had come to the theatre on a rare visit for the opening night of his latest play.

I approached the bar, to find this veteran of the theatre surrounded by many of his fans, eager to catch every word that fell from his lips in between his enjoyment of liquid refreshment. Explaining that I was the theatre's photographer, I respectfully asked if I could take his picture. "No. I can't be bothered to pose for you now," he said dismissively.

I retreated a little, but noticed there was just enough existing light, and I managed to take this unposed photograph without him being aware.

I then ordered a much needed drink to celebrate.

HARRY WHEATCROFT

Several county magazines, among them the *Birmingham Sketch*, were printed in the Nottinghamshire town of Ruddington, and it was whilst visited the area on business one day that I decided to take the opportunity of tracking down the internationally renowned rose grower Harry Wheatcroft.

Knowing that he was an extremely busy man I wasn't too optimistic about the possibility of photographing him – but nothing ventured nothing gained. I knew that he was often to be seen in the company of the Queen Mother in the London area flower shows.

However, my luck was in, and he agreed to see me. On meeting, he regarded me with suspicion, perhaps believing I was an early paparazzi! I felt he did not trust photographers but after a few moments chatting with him I had won him over and he relaxed, and later agreed to pose for me.

I was delighted when, as I left, he presented me with a cutting of his original Peace Rose, which I planted in the garden of my former home in Hartlebury where it probably still blooms

RICHARD CHAMBERLAIN

In 1969 I was asked by John Greenwood, the Artistic Director of the old Birmingham Repertory Theatre in Station Street (established by Sir Barry Jackson before the First World War), if I would be interested in photographing Shakespeare's *Hamlet*, which was shortly to be performed at the theatre. He went on to say that on a recent visit to the United States he had offered the leading role to the actor Richard Chamberlain who had become available due to the ending of the popular American TV series *Dr Kildare*. Gemma Jones, the daughter of Shakespearian actor Griffith Jones, was to play the part of Ophelia.

I readily agreed, adding that it would be a privilege to do the stills photography for this stage production. Having worked regularly for commercial television since 1957, I was well used to photographing drama productions, but looked forward to the new experience of working in a different media.

The role of Hamlet is a challenge for any actor, even more so for Richard Chamberlain, as live theatre was such a contrast to performing on the small screen, so before the technical rehearsals began I introduced myself to him and said, as I usually did on these occasions, that I was aware that his lines were more important than my photographs, and if the sound of my clicking proved a distraction in any way, he only had to indicate his disapproval and I would stop. All went well however, and by the opening night prints were on display in the small foyer of the theatre.

Gemma Jones and Richard Chamberlain were magnificent, and the production was thrilling, playing to full houses throughout the whole season.

Thus began my long association with the Birmingham Repertory Theatre; in all I worked on 189 productions. All of my photographic work on these productions is now stored at the Central Library in Birmingham, in the Shakespeare Studies Department.

1/60th F 3.5 Tri-x

NOELE GORDON

Throughout theatrical history 'upstaging' has been a serious offence, so the man behind the camera gets in front of the actors at his peril.

Crossroads, ITV's long running soap set in a motel and recorded in black and white, featured Noele Gordon as Meg Richardson, the leading female part. A regular viewer was Mary Wilson, wife of the Prime Minister Harold Wilson. He had recently resigned when she visited the new ATV studios in Bridge Street, Birmingham. It was a big occasion with the Chairman of ATV, Lew – later Lord – Grade, and other board members present .

I noticed Noele Gordon sitting next to Mrs Wilson. Noele introduced me. "Mary, this is Gus, who does a lot of our stills work," she said.

Mary Wilson had recently published a book of poetry containing a riveting article about the work of Carl Miles, the Swedish sculptor. She was pleased to hear that I had read it. I explained that a few years earlier I had visited Stockholm to photograph in Foresta Park the very sculptures she had written about, and we became completely absorbed in an animated conversation about them.

It was all too much for Noele. She had been upstaged, but not for long.

"Gus," she hissed, "your flies are undone!"

Exit a very red-faced Gus – wondering, but not daring to check.

Photo taken with my camera by another photographer 6 x 7 Mamiflex soft focus stereo flash F8 TRI

LENNY HENRY

During ATV's *New Faces* programme series, the staff photographer Des Gershon and I shared the colour and black and white stills coverage of the programme, the object of which was to discover fresh unknown talent.

A discerning panel of judges observed and listened critically to each act, and discarded those which in their opinion could not have made it on the professional stage.

Amongst the competitors, there were of course many gifted performers who would probably, given the right breaks, have a good chance of a career in the theatre. However, one performance in particular stands out in my memory. The young Lenny Henry appeared only briefly, but during his electric and hilarious appearance I had difficulty keeping my camera steady, and the studio audience were rocking in their seats.

The panel members were unanimous – Lenny had arrived.

Later, I had the privilege of working with Lenny on the effervescent *Tiswas* production, where the audience were enjoying Lenny's impersonation of the ITV news presenter Trevor Macdonald. Little did Lenny know that the real Trevor Macdonald was to creep up behind to surprise Lenny who, for a few seconds, was left speechless. His regular appearance on Chris Tarrant's lively and entertaining programme established his career, and he was soon on his way to the top.

Lenny courteously posed for my photograph (taken with a motorised Nikon) after a 'Tiswas' production outside the ATV studios in Bridge Street, Birmingham. It was difficult to select the one magic image, there were so many he was capable of.

1/250 sec F.11 Nikon Tri-x

JIMMY SAVILLE

I met the charismatic Jimmy Saville when we were both working on the 1960s television talent show *Thank Your Lucky Stars*, where I was the stills photographer and he was one of the panel of judges. Also on the panel was a very bubbly local girl, Janice Nichols, who became famous for her catch phrase "Oi'll give it foive!", (referring to the number of points awarded to contestants).

Jimmy's fondness for cigars was well known, and I couldn't help comparing his expensive brand with the inferior ones I had smoked out in the Middle East, in a forlorn attempt to keep off the innumerable flies. I wondered if I would ever be able to afford to smoke such an up-market brand myself. One day, to my surprise and delight he offered one to me - but by that time I had given up smoking, and kept it as a souvenir.

Some time later, Jimmy and I were both present at a reception given by the manufacturers of BSR Record Players where presentations were made to long serving members of staff, and I was able to surprise Jimmy by presenting him with a Panatella cigar.

I also took the opportunity to invite him to come along at a later date to the Birmingham Press Club lunch. The photograph shows him posing beside his stretch limousine on his arrival. Later, after an enjoyable lunch, we were surprised and delighted when he presented us with a cheque for £1,000 to be used towards the press fund charities.

CLIFF RICHARD

I first photographed Cliff Richard when I accompanied a party of *Birmingham Evening Despatch* readers as ABC TV's official photographer on the trip to see the *Oh Boy* show televised. On that occasion I was struck by his eyes, which had a direct and penetrating look.

I had the opportunity to photograph him again about two years later, when I was at the Birmingham Hippodrome to take some pictures to be used in the *Evening Despatch*. He impressed me greatly and I thought at the time that this polite young man had great talent and would go far. It was little wonder to me that he was the teenagers' idol. The photo which I took for Top Star Special which was used in the in the *Evening Despatch* showed he had developed into an even stronger character than in earlier photographs.

Many years later, when he was in his 50s, I asked him to come to the Birmingham Press Club lunch to receive a Personality Award. After lunch he delighted us all by giving an unaccompanied performance of his shortly to be released single *Mistletoe and Wine*.

JANICE NICHOLLS

A very popular light entertainment show in the 1960s was the BBC's *Thank Your Lucky Stars* which was recorded at the Alpha Television Studios in Birmingham on Saturday for transmission the following Sunday.

Newly released pop records were played to a panel of judges, each of whom would then award the record a mark as to how well they thought it would perform in the charts. Jimmy Saville regularly appeared on the show, and Janice Nicholls was chosen to give her opinion on the record as a teenager and an ordinary member of the public. She had a vivacious personality, and rapidly became a great favourite with viewers and judges alike. If she liked a record, she would award it five points, which came out as "Oi'll give it foive!" in Janice's local accent. This soon caught on and it became quite a catchphrase. Naturally, the producers loved this, and the programmes executives decided that Janice was a 'must'

However, one Sunday afternoon as I arrived at the studios the programme director approached me. "Have you seen Janice?" he asked. He seemed very concerned as she had not turned up for rehearsals. As I knew Janice's address in West Bromwich I volunteered to go to her home and collect her. Her mother answered the door, and explained that the usual letter confirming her appearance had not arrived, so, assuming she was not needed, she had gone to see her boyfriend performing at a pub in Brownhills. However, she didn't know exactly which one.

Looking at my watch I saw that there was an hour and a half before rehearsals began, so I sped over to Brownhills to try to locate her. Luckily, on my third attempt I found Janice, looking happy and relaxed and enjoying the music. When she spotted me she looked alarmed, and after a hasty word, within seconds we were on our way to the Aston studio. She surprised me when she told me en route that she never watched the programme when it was transmitted the following Saturday evening.

We arrived at the studio with just 15 minutes to spare before rehearsals began. All were pleased to see her. A charming girl, everyone would certainly give her 'foive'

MOHAMMED ALI

In 1984 I was asked by the Central Office of Information to cover the opening of a new sports centre in Hockley, Birmingham. The opening ceremony was to be performed by the American boxer Mohammed Ali.

I arrived in plenty of time to cover the opening, and already there were a great many people gathered outside the new building. I stood inside the glass entrance so as to have a good vantage point as the famous boxer entered. As the time approached for the opening ceremony the crowds continued to grow, until the doors looked like giving way under the sheer weight of the people pushing up against them.

Finally he arrived and the doors were opened as Mohammed Ali entered and crowds of his admirers surged in. By this time I had managed to find a vacant chair and positioned myself in what I hoped was a safe place. I was fortunate not to be knocked over by the undisciplined crowds as they swept by with their hero.

Photo opportunities became easier a little while later when this personality was on stage, from where he addressed his fans. Later, in Birmingham City Centre, I was able to obtain an unposed head and shoulders of this unique sportsman who could 'float like a butterfly and sting like a bee'.

Nikon Tri-x F.8 1/60th sec

ENOCH POWELL

During my time at the Birmingham Press Club, I invited Enoch Powell to present the prizes at the Midlands Press Photographer of the Year Awards ceremony, and after the ceremony he was presented with the Press Club tie.

It was some 14 years before we met again, when I had the privilege of photographing him seated at the desk in the library of Highbury Hall in Birmingham, the seat of the Chamberlain family, of which probably the most famous family member was Neville Chamberlain, former Prime Minister, forever remembered for the phrase 'Peace in our time' on his return from talks with Adolf Hitler in 1939.

After the photo session I asked him if he had worn the Press Club tie. Apparently he had not, and seemed embarrassed at my query! The BBC Press Officer present then told him there were several media journalists outside the room who wished to interview him. He looked at his watch and said "Alright then, ten minutes only". Soon the room was full of eager journalists anxious to speak to him. From among the many clamouring to be heard he selected a youthful journalist who put an interesting but challenging question to him. Quick as lightning he replied, and using his considerable verbal expertise (in addition to being a skilled politician, he was an eminent Greek scholar with a mind as sharp as a razor) he rapidly demolished the young journalist. There was no time left for any other questions – getting to his feet he said, "That's it now, time's up".

BERYL REID

One of the most enjoyable facets of my work in the 1950s was visiting the various theatres in the area to photograph the artists appearing in the many variety shows which were then so popular. I frequently attended the Dudley Hippodrome and the Plaza Theatre, West Bromwich, where many of the top stars of the day performed. This was the era before television held sway, and top entertainers toured the country, appearing in theatres nationwide.

Below stage at the Dudley Hippodrome was a bar, affectionately known as The Glue Pot, and here performers, stage hands, the press, photographers and a variety of people associated with the theatre congregated in a happy and convivial atmosphere. It was there that I met many of the popular entertainers of the day; personalities such as Morecambe and Wise, Tommy Cooper, Lena Horne, Ted Heath, Alma Cogan, Eve Boswell, and Ken Dodd.

A very popular performer at the local theatres at this time was the comedienne Beryl Reid, and it was when she was appearing at the Dudley Hippodrome that she agreed to pose for this photograph in her dressing room.

Sadly, during the next few years, audiences at theatres throughout the country declined, and one by one the variety theatres were forced to close - many of them becoming bingo halls. It was the end of an era for variety.

DUDLEY ZOO

From time to time, while freelancing in the 1950s with the *Midland Chronicle*, I made an occasional visit to Dudley Zoo which could often present photo opportunities.

The camera that I and most of my photographer colleagues used at that time was a British-made coupled rangefinder model called the MPP which contained double dark slides containing either 5 x 4 cut film or plates. As there was a strong camaraderie amongst us, if one of us ran out of our limited stock we could always borrow from one another.

One day, in the reptile house at Dudley Zoo, an attendant produced a live boa constrictor which we were told would not bite, but crush its victims to death by winding round them, and tightening its grip by using a tree trunk or any upright structure nearby.

Timidly touching this several feet long snake, I was surprised by its smoothness – it had not got an oily, slimy surface as I had always imagined. Almost immediately the friendly reptile began curling its way around my body, and slowly towards my neck and around my camera. Realising there was an opportunity for a good shot for another of my colleagues standing nearby, I took my already loaded double dark slide out of my camera and requested him to take my photo whilst I could still breathe!

Fortunately, the snake soon lost interest in me and started sliding off in another direction looking for another diversion.

JORDAN

In 1979 I was invited to join a press party which was travelling to Jordan in order to promote tourism in the area, which had been in decline following the six day war which had taken place in 1967 between Palestine and Israel. The aim of my visit was to reflect the beauty of the many interesting attractions in the area which would appeal to tourists.

It was my first visit to Jordan, and I was totally unprepared for the truly amazing history of this fascinating land. It was altogether one of the most memorable experiences of my career, and I certainly had plenty to talk about on my return.

On the last evening the Jordanian Tourist Authority hosted a farewell evening dinner in Amman for the press party with whom I was travelling. The Jordanian Government's information officer asked a journalist from the *Croyden Advertiser* and myself if we had enough material before we returned to England the following evening. We mentioned that when passing through Baaqa we had noticed a refugee camp and would have liked to have seen the conditions in the camp. He readily agreed, and arranged for us to be taken there the following morning. After a short journey we came upon a stretch of desert where hundreds of ex-army bell tents, albeit in a bad state of repair, were providing shelter for approximately 35,000 Palestinian refugees from the Israeli/Palestine war. Huts had also been erected to provide schoolrooms where groups of young people were being taught.

Suddenly an air raid siren sounded and immediately the children were shepherded out of the buildings, filing out quickly and obediently into slit trenches. One young man was a little bit late in obeying instructions, and was whacked with a tin tray by a grown-up to speed him on his way to safety! Looking up into the sky I was not concerned as I saw that the aircraft was a single engine plane, which was unlikely to be carrying bombs. Soon the all-clear sounded and I noticed two young girls who were in a buoyant mood as the plane disappeared from view.

I was shocked when I was told that the following winter many of the ragged tents would not withstand the severe weather and would offer little protection to the refugees, many of whom would die from hypothermia.

1/100 F 5.6 Tri-x

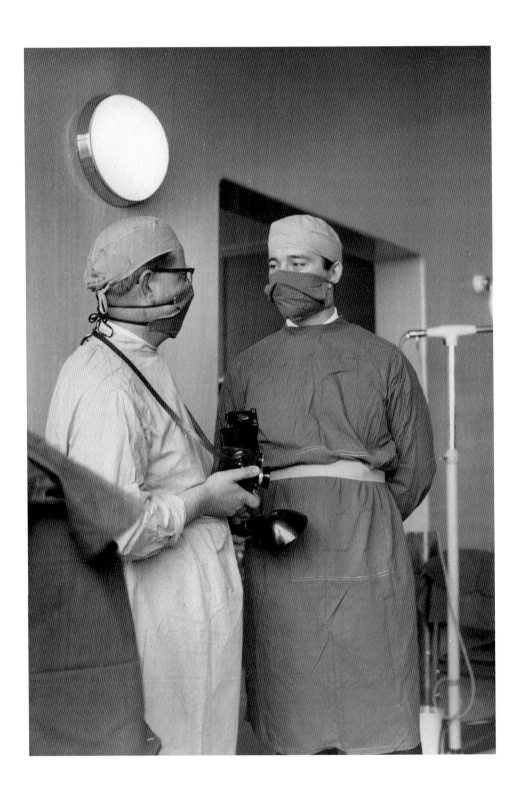

QUEEN ELIZABETH HOSPITAL

In the 1960s ABC Television presented a closed circuit television and camera with zoom lens to the Queen Elizabeth Hospital in Birmingham for use in the operating theatre for training purposes.

Shortly after the installation of the equipment I accompanied Jimmy Bake, the ABC Television Press Officer, on a visit to the hospital to take the required photographs for publicity purposes. On our arrival, we were shown into a room adjacent to the operating theatre, where medical students and nursing staff were watching on screen as an operation was being performed in the theatre nearby.

As it was a cold day outside I was wearing a heavy raglan overcoat, which I didn't bother to remove. When the operation was over the surgeon invited us into the operating theatre so that I could photograph the overall scene, and we were required to don protective gowns and headgear before being allowed inside.

As we entered the room, the sudden increase in temperature caused my glasses to steam up, and I was concerned about my camera lens also steaming up with the heat. After taking a long wide shot, which showed the camera installed high up above the operating table, trained vertically to photograph the scene below, the surgeon invited us to look at his stitching on the still unconscious patient's chest. Very impressive, but at this point, the combination of the heat and the unaccustomed sight of an operation was just too much, and we beat a hasty retreat before we were in need of resuscitation ourselves!

As I was chatting to the surgeon, another photographer borrowed my camera to take this shot of me looking more than usually rotund, with my heavy overcoat hidden under the surgical gown.

Many years later I reflected on this moment when I was undergoing a heart bypass myself at the Walsgrave Hospital in Coventry, and I felt able to put my complete trust in the skill of the surgeons performing the operation.

Photo taken by another photographer using my spare camera Tri-x Bounce flash 1/100

OLIVER LEESE

In the 1960s ATV decided to feature a programme called *The Fighting Midlands*. The programme was devised by George Bartram, and General Sir Oliver Leese was to be the consultant. He was well placed to act as an advisor for the series, having served in two world wars. During World War II Sir Oliver was second in command to General Montgomery before El Alamein and later went on to take command of the Italian campaign. Certainly a man who commanded respect.

After the war this gentleman retired to Worfield near Bridgnorth, where he pursued his hobby of growing cacti. Arrangements were made for me to go to his home to photograph him, and I was delighted when he asked me to have lunch with Lady Leese and himself. On the walls of the room were regimental plaques commemorating the battalions with which he had served.

During lunch he showed me some excellent photographs of cacti he had taken. I was surprised to learn that another of his hobbies was conducting war games with model soldiers, and a battle situation was to be seen underneath a large plastic protective cover.

I thought it would be a good idea to photograph him with this large display of soldiers. However, I pointed out that a clearer picture could be had if the protective cover was removed to avoid flash reflections. He agreed, but unfortunately, in my enthusiasm to remove the transparent cover, I clumsily bumped into the table, causing the entire display to collapse, and thus losing all the battle positions he had so painstakingly set out. He was not amused.

JERUSALEM

On a trip to Jerusalem in 1943 I visited what was then known as the Wailing Wall. On one side of a narrow lane was part of the construction of Solomon's Temple and in complete contrast, on the other side of the lane, were humble Arab dwellings. Particularly revered by those of the Jewish faith, the area is visited by many thousands each year.

I visited Jerusalem again in 1970, and went once more to see the area that had now been re-named the Western Wall. Inevitably, most places change over a period of time, but I was astonished by the change in the area surrounding Solomon's Temple. The lane and the dwellings had gone, and instead a paved incline led to this sacred place.

A partition had been erected to separate male and female worshippers, and somewhat incongruously, a guard complete with a sub-machine gun stood watch over the scene.

PEGGY ASHCROFT

Peggy Ashcroft was undoubtedly considered to be the one of the finest actresses of her generation, and I had the opportunity to take this shot when she was using the studios at BBC Pebble Mill to rehearse for a radio play.

I respectfully introduced myself, and asked if I may photograph her at a convenient moment between recordings. 'I am too busy now', she said dismissively. She then indicated her professional approach to learning her lines, and I melted unobtrusively into the background whilst the recordings were made, awaiting the opportunity to try again later.

Whilst the actress was resting between takes, a pleasant piece of music began to play which she obviously enjoyed immensely, as she became animated and radiant. Fortunately, my camera was loaded and ready to catch the memorable moment.

On 8th September 1969 she planted a mulberry tree in the garden of Great Place in Stratford-upon-Avon to commemorate the 200th anniversary of the first Shakespeare Festival at Stratford-upon-Avon, organised by David Garrick in 1769.

LEONARD WILSON

While working on one of my early photographic exhibitions *Images of the Sixties*, I arranged to photograph the Bishop of Birminham, Leonard Wilson, at his home in Harborne. In 1941 he had been consecrated as the Bishop of Singapore but unfortunately he was captured by the Japanese in 1942 and imprisoned in the dreaded Changi gaol.

I mentioned this one day in conversation with ATV's chief designer Rex Spencer, for whom I photographed many television sets for record purposes, as I knew he had also been captured at Singapore, and he expressed a wish to come along with me to meet the Bishop.

After taking the Bishop's photograph I discreetly withdrew, knowing they had many experiences to share. As I left the room, I overheard the Bishop saying in hushed tones: "They held me on a table and beat my legs with a bamboo cane until I was unconscious".

Many years later, and in 2004 I met up with Rex again and reminded him of our meeting with the Bishop. He turned to me from his wheelchair and told me that the Japanese had pulled out all of his toenails after his capture.

Rollieflex T Tri-x F8 1/100 sec

IMOGEN STUBBS

I was delighted to be asked to work on D.H.Lawrence's *The Rainbow*, a distinguished BBC Regional drama which was shot mainly in the Midlands and Nottingham areas.

I had heard the lead character Ursula was to be played by the already established actress Imogen Stubbs. On the first days shoot the set was a Victorian schoolroom of the day, with a class of young boys appropriately dressed in the clothes of that era. After reading the script I focused my camera upon a young boy at his desk who was later to be caned. Then unexpectedly a voice whispered in my ear, "Good morning, Gus". This was my first working relationship with this talented lady, who later was to marry the gifted director Trevor Nunn.

Some years later, she played the female lead as Desdemona at the RSC's The Other Place in Stratford, affectionately known as 'The Shed' by actors the world over. Willard White took the lead as Othello, whilst Iago was played by Ian Mckellan. The theatre was booked out for all the performances before the opening night. This play was memorable because it was the last production before the old 'Shed' was closed. Some years later the theatre was rebuilt on a site nearby.

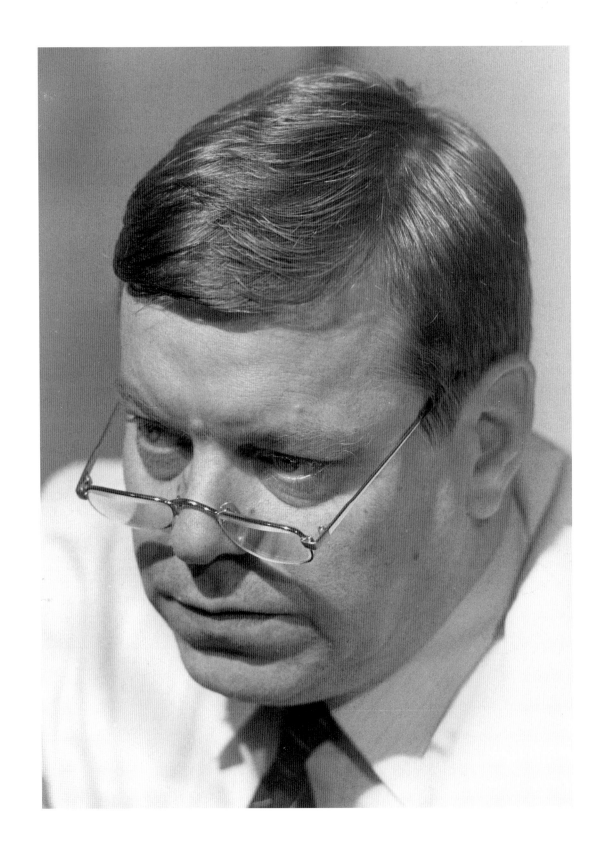

WARREN CLARKE

Warren Clarke was already an established actor when I first met him while working on the BBC televison drama production of David Lodge's *Nice Work*, set in the West Midlands.

In addition to being a fine actor, he was extremely conscientious about learning his lines properly so that, to the director's delight, Warren always seemed to get it right on the first take.

On one occasion when working on set in a disused office in the Black Country, I sat down next to him during a late pause in the shooting after midnight. Suddenly, an argument broke out among two members of the crew. Warren, who had been sitting quietly learning his lines, had been unnecessarily distracted and admonished the cause of the trouble with a few well-chosen words.

Silence followed!

LINDSAY DUNCAN

I rarely read the newspaper sports pages, a large proportion of which are filled with detailed stories of those taking part. However, the expertise that sports photographers display with their camera images indicates how much they love the game – be it tennis, rugby, cricket or football. The ability to capture 'that certain moment' derives from experience and knowledge of what is about to happen, and their 'scoresheet' benefits accordingly.

I had observed the talented actress Lindsay Duncan when she was rehearsing *Dead Head*, a BBC television drama in 1986 and considered that, if she repeated her action during the final take, I might capture the moment.

Positioning myself safely away from the sound microphones which pick up the least noise, I fitted a telephoto lens, then found a position some distance away to wait. Fortunately she repeated her moves – that certain moment had arrived and I was there to capture it.

ANTONY SHER

I was working on Malcolm Bradbury's television production of *The History Man* at the BBC's main television studio at Pebble Mill, Birmingham, in which Antony Sher, a then almost unknown actor, was playing the leading role.

On learning that he was from South Africa I thought it would break the ice if I greeted him in Afrikaans (I had lived in South Africa twice during my time in the RAF and had picked up a smattering of the language). After my initial greeting, I added, also in Afrikaans, "Your lines are far more important than my clicking camera, so please tell me to bugger off if my work throws you". I think he appreciated this, and it helped to cement a good working relationship.

Since his appearance in that early controversial production, he went on to appear in many memorable works, including his unforgettable performance as Richard III with the Royal Shakespeare Company.

To those unaware of what it takes to be an actor, I recommend his book *To Be The King*. His dedication to his art shows in the amazing amount of research he did into the part before he had even been formally selected for the lead. Not only is the book a very enjoyable read, he also did the sketches and illustrations, displaying still more of his many talents.

WHITWICK COLLIERY

From time to time I was called on to do shots on location for drama productions, which occasionally turned out to be more dramatic than I was expecting. On one such occasion, ATV's property department needed a picture for visual reference in its production of D. H. Lawrence's *Sons and Lovers*. The camera viewpoint had to be shot over an actor's shoulder, showing miners at work at the coal face and I was called upon to take the pictures.

On arriving at Whitwick colliery, we were fitted up with miners' lamps, suitable clothing and knee pads, prior to descending in the cage into the dark depths of the mine. After what seemed an eternity we emerged from the cage with the miners into what seemed like another world.

I could see nothing in the first few seconds, but once my eyes adjusted to the darkness I saw ahead of us a pathway with a very low ceiling. Our lamps illuminated the way as we trekked forward, keeping our heads down, until we eventually came to the working area where the miners crouched, gouging away at the coal in a very low and confined space. To prevent the roof from falling in, hydraulic ramps had been fitted into place, which creaked ominously overhead every so often, sounds which were disturbing to say the least.

I was not allowed to use flash because of the danger in the underground circumstances, so the pictures were taken with aid of the miners who, on my instructions, directed their lamps on to the actor and the surrounding area. Eventually, having completed my work, I was looking forward to an early release from this man-made hell when the Underground Manager standing nearby was suddenly given an urgent message that the apparently safe tunnel we had earlier walked through had caved in, bringing down the walls which were now a mangle of wood and steel supports.

Calmly telling us to stay where we were, the Underground Manager went ahead of us with his inspection lamp and, slithering cautiously along through the destroyed tunnel area, he checked to see whether there was a possible escape route through the tangle of ironwork and broken wood to the exit some 30 yards away.

"It's alright to come through," he shouted reassuringly to us. Squirming low down on our bellies, we crawled slowly towards the safe area, my cameras dragging behind me as I proceeded. A miner following me shouted sharply, "You'd better keep your bloody arse down sir, or you will bring more down on top of us!"

Some time later, in the miners' canteen, I enjoyed the best cup of tea ever. My respect for all those who work underground has never diminished.

The Author

Born in Northumberland in 1921, Willoughby 'Gus' Gullachsen's career as a photographer began nearly 70 years ago. After war service in the RAF as a photographer in South Africa, India and Iraq (pictured above in 1945), he moved to the West Midlands where he worked as a freelance photographer for ABC Television (later ATV), *TV Times* and the BBC. During the next 50 years he photographed 189 productions for the Birmingham Repertory Theatre, many RSC productions at his home town of Stratford-upon-Avon, and was the unit photographer for BBC Drama for 22 years.

In addition, 'Gus' has had many exhibitions of his work staged at venues in Birmingham and Stratford, the most recent being his *Images Of The Sixties* at the Waterhall Gallery of Modern Art in Birmingham in 2005. Many of his photographs are now held among the collections in Birmingham's Central Library.